FABULOUS GLUTEN-FREE BAKING

Gluten-Free Recipes and Clever Tips for Pizza, Cupcakes, Pancakes, and Much More

Smilla Luuk

PHOTOGRAPHY: Jenny Grimsgård

GRAPHIC & ILLUSTRATIONS: Katy Kimbell

Translated by Gun Penhoat

Skyhorse Publishing

CONTENTS

Hello!

Since I was four, I've wanted to open up a café and call it "Sweetie Pie." As a little kid, I often baked when I got home from after-school day care, and at one point I really did open the Sweetie Pie Café—in the middle of my family's living room. My maternal and paternal grandparents were my first customers.

One year later, I was diagnosed with celiac disease, which means that I suffer from gluten intolerance. Fortunately at the time I didn't quite understand what that signified, or else I might have given up baking entirely. Instead I kept on going, and while my condition presented a few new challenges, with my parents' support, I was able to discover a whole new world that was opening up for me.

In 2010, after seven years of baking from both trusted and adapted recipes (with varying degrees of success), I started a blog called *glutenfrittliv.se*. I recorded all my recipes on it and blogged about life as someone who is gluten intolerant, or a *Gluten*, as I usually call it.

Today, I'm seventeen years old, and one of my biggest dreams has come true: you are holding in your hands my very first cookbook. It's chock-full of my most successful gluten-free recipes, as well as tips and tricks on how to find your way through the gluten-filled jungle. It doesn't have to be tricky—you can enjoy just as many (if not more!) tasty baked goods as anyone else.

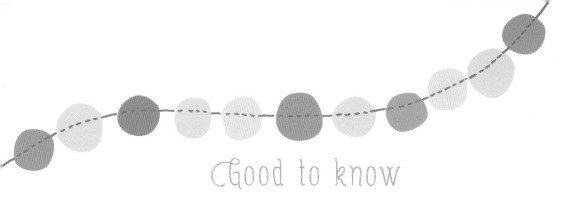

Good to know

1 There are many different brands of gluten-free baking mixes available on the market, and they don't all work the same way. I prefer to use mixes that don't contain psyllium husk; I add this ingredient separately if I feel it is needed. Try different mixes until you find one you like, or try my homemade version:

Smilla's Gluten-free Flour Mix:

> 1⅓ cups (150 g) corn flour (finest grade)
> 1 cup (150 g) rice flour
> 1¼ cups (200 g) potato flour
>
> Just a smidgen under 1 tbsp (6 g) guar gum
> 1 tsp baking powder

Mix everything thoroughly in a bowl and use whenever a recipe calls for "gluten-free flour mix."

2 *Sifting* is done by putting dry ingredients into a fine-mesh sieve and carefully shaking it over a bowl or a cake in order to remove any lumps or large particles.

3 When I bake, I usually make a double batch of frosting and/or filling because I feel that many recipes are a bit stingy with them. With the recipes in this book, however, you won't have to double them because I've already taken care of that for you! After all, the frosting and filling are the stars of the show, aren't they?

4 Remember that the liquid you use to make your dough needs to be lukewarm before you add yeast to it. If the liquid is too warm it will kill the yeast, and if it's too cold the dough will not rise. It is therefore critical that your liquid be tepid so your sweet rolls don't end up flat as pancakes!

5 "Work additional flour into the dough if it's too loose or sticky." Follow this advice cautiously, and only if your dough is so loose that it's absolutely impossible to shape. Gluten-free dough is always stickier than dough containing gluten, and the more flour mix you add to the dough, the drier and tougher the baked goods will be.

6 Keep in mind that all ovens have slight discrepancies in temperature and can therefore produce different-looking results. Baking times can also vary from oven to oven.

Special note about measurements: Cups have been added for ease of the user. Some of the measurements have been rounded off, but every effort has been made to keep the measurements as precise as possible. In some cases, such as when baking macarons, it's better to weigh the ingredients for a more exact amount. If you do not have a scale at home, measure with care. However, using the measurements will still yield fun and delicious gluten-free treats.

Soft Baked Goods

I'll start off this book with my best recipes for sweet and soft baked goods—the kinds of treats you bake in the afternoon, or in the middle of the night if you're a night owl like me. My favorite recipe is for Love's *Yummy Nibbles*—they're absolutely heavenly!

Vanilla or Chocolate Muffins with Chocolate Fudge Filling

makes 24 large muffins

YOU'LL NEED:

3 large eggs
1¼ cups (240 g) granulated sugar
2 tbsp vanilla extract + 2 tbsp granulated sugar or 3 tbsp cocoa powder
1⅔ cups (240 g) gluten-free flour mix
2 tsp baking powder
½ tsp salt
½ cup (100 g) butter
3⅓ fl oz (100 ml) milk

Filling:

1 bag chocolate-covered Dumle toffee or Rolos*, or 4 oz (100 g) good-quality baking chocolate

Individual muffin baking cups/molds

HOW TO'S:

1. Preheat a convection oven to 400°F (200°C).
2. Place muffin cups onto a cookie sheet. Use sturdier muffin cups or double them up to prevent the batter from bubbling over during baking.
3. Beat the eggs and sugar with a handheld electric mixer until the batter is light and airy.
4. In a separate bowl and using a fork, combine the 2 tbsp vanilla extract and 2 tbsp sugar (for vanilla muffins) or cocoa powder (for chocolate muffins) with the gluten-free flour mix, baking powder, and salt.
5. Place the butter in a microwave-safe bowl and melt it in the microwave for 1 minute on medium power.
6. Pour butter, milk, and the flour mix into the egg/sugar batter. With the electric mixer on its lowest setting, beat the mix until you have a smooth batter without any lumps.
7. *If you want to include chocolate chunks in the muffins: Coarsely chop the chocolate and mix the pieces into the batter.*
8. Fill the muffin molds to about half full. If you fill them too much, the batter might bubble over in the oven.
9. *If you're making muffins with Dumle toffee or Rolos: Push one piece of candy into each muffin.*
10. Bake the muffins in the middle of the oven for about 15 minutes; check them with a toothpick to see if they're ready. The toothpick should come out clean, slightly moist but without any crumbs or batter on it.

* Dumle is chocolate candy with a toffee center that is popular in Sweden and Finland. Rolos are a good substitute if you can't find Dumle at Whole Foods or your local specialty store.

Hazelnut Muffins with Milk Chocolate

makes about 15 muffins

YOU'LL NEED:

5¼ oz (150 g) hazelnuts (filberts)
2 large eggs
1 cup (190 g) granulated sugar
1 cup (150 g) gluten-free flour mix
1½ tsp baking powder
1 tbsp cocoa powder
a pinch of salt
¼ cups (50 g) butter
1⅓ cups (50 g) milk chocolate
¼ cup (50 ml) milk

Muffin cups / paper molds

HOW TO'S:

1. Preheat a convection oven to 400°F (200°C).
2. Place the muffin cups onto a cookie sheet. Use sturdier muffin cups or double them up to prevent the batter from bubbling over during baking.
3. Grind the hazelnuts in a coffee grinder or Magic Bullet-type blender. You'll want a coarse powder.
4. Beat the eggs and sugar with a handheld electric mixer until the batter is light and airy.
5. Using a fork, combine the gluten-free flour mix with baking powder, cocoa powder, salt, and the hazelnut powder in a separate bowl.
6. In a microwave-safe bowl, melt the butter and milk chocolate together for about a minute in the microwave on medium power.
7. Pour the flour mix, butter/chocolate mix, and the milk into the egg/sugar batter. With the electric mixer set on its lowest speed, mix until you have a smooth batter without any lumps.
8. Fill the muffin molds halfway. If you make them too full, they might bubble over in the oven.
9. Bake the muffins in the middle of the oven for about 15 minutes; check them with a toothpick to see if they are ready. The toothpick should come out moist but without any crumbs or batter attached.

When I was a little kid I was extremely cautious about everything I could and could not eat. I was so used to inspecting the ingredients list on food labels that one day my dad found me in the kitchen, reading the label on a DVD to see if the film contained any gluten . . .

Frostings

Frostings will take your muffins to a whole new level—they'll become cupcakes!

CHOCOLATE FROSTING

YOU'LL NEED:

3½ oz (100 g) Philadelphia cream cheese
2 tbsp Nutella chocolate hazelnut spread
2 tbsp chocolate fudge sauce
⅔ cup (60 g) confectioner's sugar
1 tbsp cocoa powder

HOW TO'S:

1. Place all ingredients into a bowl.
2. Mix until you have a smooth cream. You can use a fork, an immersion blender, or a handheld electric mixer.
3. Pipe or spread the frosting on your muffins.

VANILLA FROSTING

YOU'LL NEED:

7 oz (200 g) Philadelphia cream cheese
¾ cup (75 g) confectioner's sugar
4 tsp vanilla extract + 4 tsp granulated sugar
¼ lemon, juiced
a few drops of food coloring (optional)

HOW TO'S:

1. Place all ingredients into a bowl.
2. Mix until you have a smooth cream. You can use a fork, an immersion blender, or a handheld electric mixer.
3. Pipe or spread the frosting on your muffins.

WHITE CHOCOLATE FROSTING

YOU'LL NEED:

¾ cup (100 g) white chocolate
7 oz (200 g) Philadelphia cream cheese
¾ cup (75 g) confectioner's sugar
4 tsp vanilla extract + 4 tsp granulated sugar
¼ lemon, juiced
a few drops of food coloring (optional)

HOW TO'S:

1. Melt the white chocolate in a microwave-safe bowl, in the microwave. Stir the chocolate every 30 seconds to prevent it from scorching.
2. Place all ingredients into a bowl.
3. Mix until you have a smooth cream. You can use a fork, an immersion blender, or a handheld electric mixer.
4. Pipe or spread the frosting on your muffins.

Tips! If you'd like different colored frostings on your cupcakes, make a batch of the vanilla frosting or the white chocolate frosting. Divide the frosting into different bowls and stir in a few drops of food coloring into each bowl. There are many fun colors to try—if you're bored with ordinary shades, try a mix of, say, blue and green, to get a turquoise-tinted frosting.

From the top: *chocolate frosting, white chocolate frosting, vanilla frosting with green food coloring, vanilla frosting with blue food coloring, vanilla frosting with red food coloring.*

Sticky Fudge Cake

makes about 8 large or 12 small servings

YOU'LL NEED:
½ cup (100 g) butter
2 large eggs
1½ cup (285 g) granulated sugar
1 cup (150 g) gluten-free flour mix
¼ cup (20 g) cocoa powder
1½ tsp vanilla extract + 1½ tsp sugar
¼ tsp salt
2 heaping tbsp Nutella hazelnut
  chocolate spread
gluten-free flour, and butter for the
  baking pan

Garnish:
Confectioner's sugar

HOW TO'S:
1. Preheat a convection oven to 400°F (200°C).
2. Grease a 9½" (24 cm) diameter springform pan, and dust it with flour.
3. Place the butter in a microwave-safe bowl and melt it for 1 minute in the microwave on medium power.
4. Beat the eggs and sugar with a handheld electric mixer until they are light and fluffy.
5. Combine the gluten-free flour mix with cocoa powder, vanilla extract and sugar, salt, Nutella, and the melted butter. Beat with a mixer or with a spoon until you have a smooth batter.
6. Pour the batter into the prepared spring form pan.
7. Bake the cake in the middle of the oven for about 15 minutes, if you want the cake to be runny in the center, or 25 minutes if you want it almost baked through. Test the cake's doneness with a toothpick—I think the consistency is perfect after 15 minutes: it's sticky but has a crust on top and around the side.
8. Dust the cake with confectioner's sugar and serve it with some whipped cream and raspberries.

Tips! The best way to dust a cake with confectioner's sugar is to pour some sugar into a tea strainer and shake the sugar through the strainer over the cake. If you want to make a decorative pattern on top of the cake, use a paper stencil.

Heavenly Chocolate–Smothered Brownies

makes 24 large or 48 small nibbles

YOU'LL NEED:

⅔ cup (150 g) butter
5 fl oz (150 ml) water
2 large eggs
1½ cup (285 g) granulated sugar
2 cups (270 g) gluten-free flour mix
2½ tsp baking powder
2 tsp vanilla extract + 2 tsp sugar
½ cup (40 g) cocoa powder

Glaze:

½ cup (100 g) butter (don't use liquid
    butter or else the glaze will not set)
1½ cup (240 g) confectioner's sugar
4 tbsp cocoa powder
4 tsp vanilla extract + 4 tsp granulated sugar
4 tbsp Nutella hazelnut chocolate spread
1¾ fl oz (50 ml) coffee
1¾ fl oz (50 ml) water

Garnish:

Shredded coconut

HOW TO'S:

1. Preheat a convection oven to 430°F (225°C).
2. Line parchment paper along a brownie pan with high sides.
3. Melt the butter in a saucepan.
4. Add the water to the butter and bring to a boil. Put a lid on the saucepan to prevent steam from escaping. Keep a close watch on the saucepan, as its contents could boil over very easily.
5. When the butter water starts to bubble, remove the saucepan from the burner and let it cool.
6. Place eggs, vanilla extract, and sugar in a bowl.
7. Beat the eggs, vanilla extract, and sugar for a few minutes with a handheld electric mixer to get a very light and airy batter.
8. Place the gluten-free flour mix, baking powder, and cocoa powder in a separate bowl.
9. Stir the dry ingredients with a fork until the mix looks like a pale brown powder.
10. Using a sieve, sift the flour mix into the egg batter by shaking the sieve with the flour mix over the egg batter. That way the flour mix blends into the batter without any lumps.
11. Pour the butter water into the egg/flour batter.
12. With an electric hand mixer on its lowest setting, beat carefully until you have a smooth batter.
13. Pour the batter into the prepared brownie pan.
14. Bake the cake in the middle of the oven for about 10 minutes. Test it with a toothpick to gauge when the cake is ready. The toothpick should come out moist but not have any trace of crumbs or batter.

Make the glaze while the cake is in the oven!

1. Melt the butter in a saucepan or in the microwave.
2. Pour in the confectioner's sugar, cocoa powder, 4 tsp vanilla extract and 4 tsp sugar, Nutella, coffee, and water. If you don't like coffee, just leave it out and use the same amount of water instead.
3. Beat with a handheld electric mixer until you have a smooth glaze.
4. Let the glaze cool a little.
5. Once the cake has cooled off completely, apply the glaze. Spread it on evenly and finish with a generous coating of shredded coconut. Cut the cake into squares and serve!

Yum!

Cinnamon Buns

makes 20 buns

YOU'LL NEED:
⅓ cup (75 g) butter
1 cup (250 ml) milk
1 oz (25 g) fresh yeast (or 2 tsp active dry yeast)
1 tbsp whole psyllium husks, unflavored
3 cups (420 g) gluten-free flour mix
2½ tsp ground cardamom
½ tsp salt
⅓ cup (65 g) granulated sugar
¼ cup (50 ml) filmjölk (available at Whole
    Foods or specialty stores)*—*I know it may
    seem like a strange ingredient to include
    here, but it makes the buns very moist and
    adds a nice tasty tang to the dough.*
1¾ fl oz (50 ml) light syrup
*Additional gluten-free flour mix to work
    the dough*

Paper baking molds

Buttercream filling:
⅔ cup (150 g) butter, at room temperature
¾ cup (142 g) granulated sugar
3 tbsp ground cinnamon

Glazing:
1 egg
Pearl sugar

HOW TO'S:
1. Melt the butter in a microwave-safe bowl in the microwave, or in a saucepan on the stovetop.
2. Pour the milk into the melted butter to make a lukewarm liquid—this means that it won't feel too warm or too cold when tested with the tip of a finger.
3. Crumble the fresh yeast into the butter/milk liquid. (If using dried yeast instead, follow instructions on the packet.**)
4. Add in the psyllium husk, mix thoroughly with a fork, and then let rise for 10 minutes.
5. In a separate bowl, pour in the gluten-free flour mix, cardamom, salt, sugar, buttermilk, syrup, and butter/milk liquid. Work the dough vigorously with a handheld electric mixer or a standing mixer, either fitted with dough hooks, for at least 5 minutes. It's very important to work the dough long enough to make it elastic and springy.
6. Cover the dough with a kitchen towel and let it rise for 50 minutes.
7. Prepare the filling right before the rise time is up: Mix butter, sugar, and cinnamon in a bowl. Using a handheld electric mixer, beat until you have a smooth paste.
8. Preheat a convection oven to 430°F (225°C).
9. Dust a baking board with gluten-free flour mix.
10. Knead the dough lightly once it has finished rising. It should feel slightly sticky to the touch.
11. Roll out the dough with a rolling pin to form a thin rectangle.
12. Spread the buttercream filling evenly over the rectangle.
13. Roll up the rectangle and slice it evenly to make 20 pieces.
14. Place each piece of dough into a cupcake wrapper. Pat the pieces to flatten and widen them a little. They'll rise in height in the heat of the oven.
15. Whip the egg with a fork and brush the buns with the egg wash. Sprinkle the top with pearl sugar.
16. Bake the buns in the middle of the oven for approximately 7 minutes.

* If you can't find filmjölk, yogurt or cultured buttermilk is a good substitute.
** Dry yeast isn't handled the same way as fresh yeast and sometimes the instructions from different makers vary, so it is best to follow the instructions on the packet very carefully.

Semlor–Mardi Gras Cream Buns

makes 6 buns

YOU'LL NEED:

¼ cup (50 g) butter
1 cup (250 ml) milk
1 oz (25 g) fresh yeast (or 2 tsp active dry yeast)
¼ cup (48 g) granulated sugar
½ tsp salt
2 tsp ground cardamom
2½ cups (360 g) gluten-free flour mix

1 egg for glazing

Filling:

1¼ cup (300 ml) heavy whipping cream
7 oz (200 g) almond paste

Confectioner's sugar for decoration

HOW TO'S:

1. Melt the butter in a microwave-safe bowl for about 1 minute in a microwave on medium power.
2. Pour the milk into the melted butter so the liquid becomes lukewarm; it should neither feel too cold nor too warm when you use your fingertip to test it. You might have to heat the butter/milk mixture a little to reach the right temperature, which should be about 99°F (37°C).
3. If using fresh yeast, crumble it into the liquid. If using dried yeast, follow instructions on the packet.
4. In a separate bowl, mix sugar, salt, cardamom, gluten-free flour, and the butter/milk liquid.
5. Work the dough with a handheld electric mixer or a standing mixer fitted with dough hooks until the dough is cleared away from the sides of the bowl. This will take a few minutes. If the dough still feels too wet, you can add a *tiny* amount of gluten-free flour mix.
6. Cover the dough with a kitchen towel and let it rise for about 30 minutes. During this time, line a cookie sheet with parchment paper.
7. Once the dough has risen, knead it a little more and then divide it into 6 even pieces.
8. Roll each piece of dough into a round bun and place it on the prepared cookie sheet.
9. Preheat a convection oven to 475°F (250°C).
10. Let the buns rise a second time, under the kitchen towel, for 20 minutes.
11. Crack an egg into a glass and whip it with a fork to mix the yolk and the egg white thoroughly to make an egg wash.
12. Once the buns have stopped rising, brush on the egg wash and bake the buns in the middle of the oven for approximately 7 minutes.
13. While the buns are baking, grate the almond paste with a grater.
14. When the buns have turned golden brown, remove them from the oven and let them cool.
15. Slice the top of the buns off to make lids, and make a small dent in both the bun and the lid.
16. Add some grated almond paste to the hole in the bun, and reserve a little for the whipped cream.
17. Whip the cream until soft peaks form, and mix in the rest of the grated almond paste.
18. Place dollops of whipped cream in the bottom sections of the buns, and replace the lids on top of the whipped cream.
19. Finish by sifting confectioner's sugar over the buns with a tea strainer and a paper stencil.

Party Time

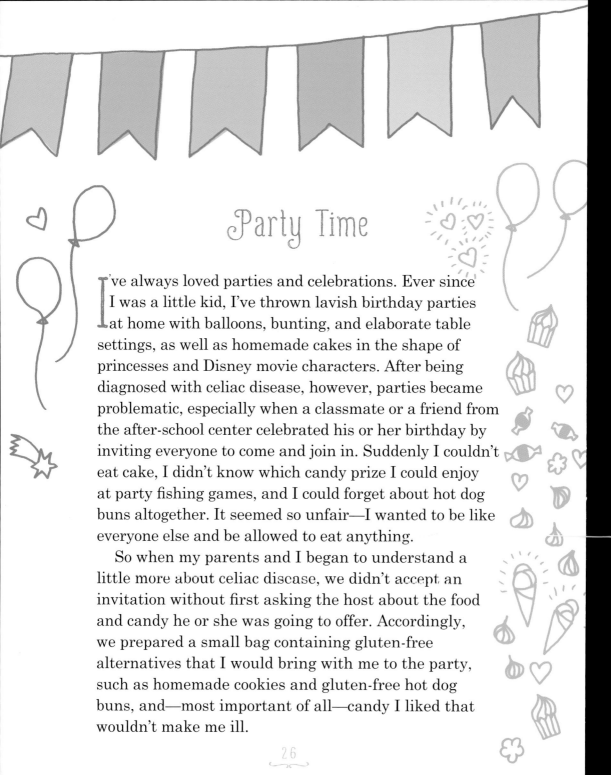

I've always loved parties and celebrations. Ever since I was a little kid, I've thrown lavish birthday parties at home with balloons, bunting, and elaborate table settings, as well as homemade cakes in the shape of princesses and Disney movie characters. After being diagnosed with celiac disease, however, parties became problematic, especially when a classmate or a friend from the after-school center celebrated his or her birthday by inviting everyone to come and join in. Suddenly I couldn't eat cake, I didn't know which candy prize I could enjoy at party fishing games, and I could forget about hot dog buns altogether. It seemed so unfair—I wanted to be like everyone else and be allowed to eat anything.

So when my parents and I began to understand a little more about celiac disease, we didn't accept an invitation without first asking the host about the food and candy he or she was going to offer. Accordingly, we prepared a small bag containing gluten-free alternatives that I would bring with me to the party, such as homemade cookies and gluten-free hot dog buns, and—most important of all—candy I liked that wouldn't make me ill.

Today I don't feel the same pressure to fit in by eating exactly the same foods as the other people. If I've been invited to dinner or to a party, I usually let the hosts know what I can eat: a meringue torte, for example, instead of a princess cake filled with whipped cream and covered in almond paste. If they've already decided to serve spaghetti carbonara as a main course, then I'll bring my own spaghetti that I can prepare at the same time. I don't want to embarrass my friends by turning up my nose at their food simply because I haven't told them I can't eat gluten.

My best tips for when invited somewhere:
Educate your friends! It might feel a bit like an unimportant step or even a hassle, but it does help enormously. Uninformed people are never as accommodating as those who know and understand exactly what it means to be gluten intolerant.

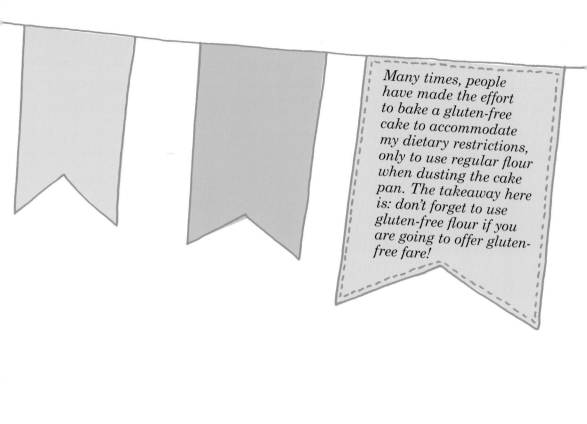

Many times, people have made the effort to bake a gluten-free cake to accommodate my dietary restrictions, only to use regular flour when dusting the cake pan. The takeaway here is: don't forget to use gluten-free flour if you are going to offer gluten-free fare!

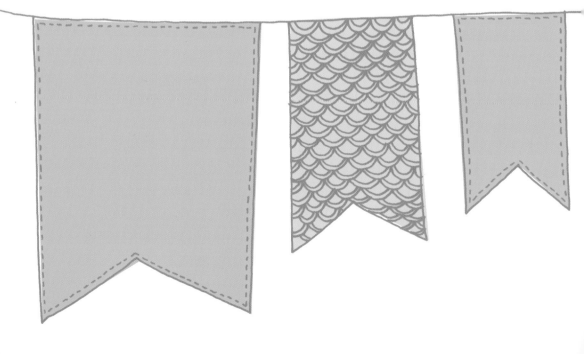

LAYER CAKES

We eat with both our mouths and eyes, which is perhaps why cakes are some of the most delectable edibles—they're both delicious and incredibly beautiful. My very best recipe in this chapter is probably the first one.

Luscious Heart Meringue Cake

approximately 6 large or 12 small slices

YOU'LL NEED:

4 large egg whites
1¼ cup (240 g) granulated sugar
¼ tsp salt
½ cup (70 g) dark chocolate
1¼ cups (300 ml) heavy whipping cream

Lots of fresh raspberries

HOW TO'S:

1. Preheat a convection oven to 300°F (150°C).
2. Line two baking sheets with parchment paper.
3. Draw two hearts—as large as the paper will allow—with a black marker on each of the two sheets of parchment. Turn the written sides down to face the baking sheet.
4. Separate the eggs into yolks and whites. Pour the egg whites into a stainless steel bowl.
5. Add the salt and the sugar to the bowl.
6. Fill a saucepan half full with water and bring it to a boil.
7. Lower the heat so the water is just barely bubbling. Place the bowl with the egg white/sugar mixture on top of the saucepan. It'll fit kind of like a lid. It might seem a bit awkward at first, but you are going to whip up a meringue over a water bath, which will keep the meringue at a constant heat.
8. Whip the egg white/sugar mixture until a thermometer registers 149°F (65°C). If you haven't got a thermometer, whip the egg whites until they've thickened and don't feel gritty when you taste test them.
9. Remove the bowl from the saucepan. Beat the contents for 5 more minutes with a handheld electric mixer, until the mixture has cooled somewhat.
10. Melt the chocolate in the microwave and drizzle it into the mixture.
11. Fold the chocolate into the mixture so it leaves streaks. Fold a little at a time, and very carefully, or the mixture will lose its airiness, deflate, and become runny.
12. Dot the mixture onto the sheets of parchment paper, using the drawn paper hearts as your guide.
13. Bake both sheets at the same time, and rotate them every 15 minutes to ensure they're evenly baked.
14. Let the layers cool.
15. Whip the cream until it's fairly stiff.
16. Place a dollop of cream onto a cake platter as "glue," and then place the first cooled meringue layer on top of it.
17. Spread an even layer of whipped cream and set raspberries into the cream.
18. Place the next meringue layer on top, and repeat with cream and raspberries.
19. Repeat with a third and even a fourth layer. Finish the cake with a layer of cream and raspberries.

Tips! It can be difficult to cut through all the layers without the cake collapsing. One easy way to serve the cake is to cut each layer separately.

Pavlova

This cake is absolutely perfect for someone who likes fresh berries as much as I do! I usually use strawberries, blackberries, raspberries, blueberries, and cherries, as well as red and black currants. I recommend using fresh berries here, as frozen berries will thaw and become too watery, which will end up soaking through and ruining the layer of meringue.

YOU'LL NEED:
6 egg whites
2 cups (425 g) granulated sugar
⅜ tsp salt
1 cup (250 ml) heavy whipping cream
4 passion fruits
Lots of fresh berries! The more the better!

HOW TO'S:
1. Preheat a convection oven to 300°F (150°C).
2. Separate the eggs into yolks and whites. Pour the egg whites into a stainless steel bowl.
3. Add the sugar and salt to the egg whites.
4. Fill a saucepan half full of water and bring it to a boil.
5. Lower the heat so the water simmers down, that is, to just barely bubbling. Place the bowl with the egg white/sugar mixture on top of the saucepan. It'll fit kind of like a lid. It might seem a bit awkward at first, but you are going to whip up a meringue over a water bath, which will keep the meringue at a constant heat.
6. Whip the egg white/sugar mixture until a thermometer registers 149°F (65°C). If you haven't got a thermometer, whip the egg whites until they've thickened and they don't feel gritty when you taste test them. This might take a little while.
7. Remove the bowl from the saucepan. Beat the contents for another 5 minutes with a handheld electric mixer, until the mixture has cooled down a little.
8. Line a baking sheet with parchment paper. Dot out the meringue mixture in a large, round layer. Try to shape the layer so it has a taller outside rim.
9. Bake the meringue on the middle rack of the oven for approximately 1 hour.
10. Remove the meringue from the oven and let it cool completely. It doesn't matter if there is a crack or two—they will be fully covered when you pile on the fruit and berries.
11. When the layer of meringue is completely cool to the touch, whip the cream and spread it thinly over the meringue, then load it up with berries, and lastly, spoon over passion fruit seeds.

You don't have to hull the fruit before decorating the cake. The Pavlova will look more natural and vibrant if you leave the stalks on the berries.

Princess Cake

makes approximately 20 servings

YOU'LL NEED:
⅓ cup (70 g) butter
3⅓ fl oz (100 ml) water
2 large eggs
1 cup (190 g) granulated sugar
1¼ cup (180 g) gluten-free flour mix
2 tsp baking powder
1 tbsp vanilla extract +1 tbsp sugar
The zested peel of ½ lemon
Butter and gluten-free flour for the cake
pan

Filling:
* 1⅓ cup (400 g) strawberry jam, preferably with some chunks of strawberry
* 1 packet of gluten-free pudding mix (look for a gluten-free powder to mix with milk)
* Milk for the pudding

Decoration:
1 pre-packaged (green) sheet of marzipan.*
A block of pink marzipan
Confectioner's sugar

HOW TO'S:
1. Preheat a convection oven to 350°F (175°C).
2. Butter and dust a 9½" inch (24 cm) diameter springform cake pan.
3. Put the butter and water in a saucepan and bring to a boil. The butter will melt and the water will start to bubble. Check carefully to keep it from boiling over.
4. With a handheld electric mixer, whip the eggs and sugar until light and fluffy.
5. In a separate bowl blend flour mix, baking powder, and vanilla extract and sugar.
6. Wash the lemon, dry it, and grate the peel; fold it into the egg mixture.
7. Carefully mix the egg batter, the flour mix, and the butter water together. It's important to be gentle to avoid deflating the air in the batter.
8. Pour the batter into the cake pan.
9. Bake on the lowest rack of the oven for approximately 40 minutes. Test that the cake is done by inserting a toothpick into it. The toothpick should come out moist but free of crumbs or batter.
10. While the cake is in the oven, prepare the pudding by following the instructions on the package. Place the pudding in the refrigerator to set firmly.
11. Sculpt a rose with the pink marzipan.
12. Once the cake is ready, let it cool thoroughly. If you place it in the refrigerator 30 minutes before cutting it in two layers, it won't make as many crumbs.
13. Cut the cake in half to make two layers.
14. Spread the jam on one layer, place the other layer on top, and spread the pudding over it. Mount a little more pudding in the middle of the cake to give it a round, dome-like shape.
15. Layer the sheet of green marzipan on top of the cake and cut off the excess marzipan along the edges. Save the excess marzipan to make rose leaves.
16. Dust the cake with confectioner's sugar and decorate with the rose and the leaves.

* Be sure to check the list of ingredients carefully! Some marzipan is rolled out with wheat flour.

To make a marzipan rose:

Cut six equal-sized pieces of pink marzipan. Shape one piece into a cone. Roll and flatten the other pieces to make them into very thin leaves. Place them around the main cone, one by one. Fan out the leaves a little at the top. When all leaves are in place, pinch them together at the bottom and tweak them until the rose looks pretty. If the marzipan becomes sticky and difficult to work with, dust your fingers or the marzipan with confectioner's sugar to make it easier to shape.

Make rose leaves out of the leftover green marzipan by rolling a few pieces into teardrop shapes and flattening them. To make the leaves more realistic, take a knife and carefully trace some veins on top of the leaves.

Grandma's Chocolate Cake

makes approximately 12 pieces

YOU'LL NEED:
14 oz (400 g) almond paste
4 egg whites

Chocolate cream filling:
½ cup (125 g) dark or milk chocolate
⅔ cup (150 g) butter
4 large egg yolks
¾ cup (145 g) granulated sugar
3⅓ oz (100 ml) heavy whipping cream
Pink and green marzipan

HOW TO'S:
1. Preheat a convection oven to 350°F (175°C) and line two baking sheets with parchment paper.
2. Using a dinner plate as a guide, draw one circle on each of the sheets of parchment.
3. Butter the two circles to prevent the layers of cake from getting stuck to them.
4. Grate the almond paste coarsely.
5. Beat the egg whites until stiff peaks form (To test: if you turn the bowl upside down, the egg whites should stay in the bowl.) Fold the grated almond paste into the egg whites.
6. Dot this mixture onto the pieces of parchment and spread it to fill in the two drawn circles.
7. Bake the two sheets together for about 20 minutes, swapping their rack positions about halfway through the baking time.
8. Carefully loosen the layers of cake from the parchment paper as soon as they come out of the oven. Let them cool thoroughly.

Chocolate cream filling:
1. Chop the chocolate finely and cut the butter into small cubes.
2. Place yolks, sugar, and cream in a saucepan and stir with a spoon while the mixture slowly heats up over low heat.
3. Heat the mixture until it starts to simmer—this means there are small bubbles, but DO NOT LET IT COME TO A BOIL.
4. Once the mixture has begun simmering, set your kitchen timer for 5 minutes. Stir constantly during these 5 minutes or until the cream starts to thicken. Remove the pan from the heat.
5. Place the chopped chocolate into the cream and let it melt completely.
6. Pour the mixture into another bowl and let it cool a little.
7. Add in the cubed butter. Stir carefully to make a smooth and shiny cream.
8. Leave the cream in the refrigerator to set; it should become chilled, thick, and smooth.
9. While the cream is setting, make the marzipan roses. See instructions on how to do this on page 35.
10. Spread chocolate cream over one layer of cake. Place the next layer of cake on top, spread with more chocolate cream, and decorate with roses and leaves, with maybe a dusting of confectioner's sugar to finish.

Tips! This cake is perfect for freezing. I cut and freeze it in individual portions, so when I crave a piece I can simply defrost one slice instead of the entire cake.

When traveling

Traveling can sometimes be a challenge for those who are gluten intolerant. The first time I went abroad I packed my own pasta, bread, and breakfast cereals to be absolutely sure I had access to gluten-free food. It was intended as a safety net, but in the end I had to throw most of it away because the cereal flakes and bread crumbled into a mess by the time I was on the plane. Plus, we didn't have access to a kitchen so we had no place to cook the pasta. Instead I ate in restaurants like everybody else, and at breakfast I ate only things I knew wouldn't make me ill. I have traveled quite a lot since that first trip and have been in different hotels. Once I stayed at an all-inclusive resort where all food was included in the holiday package, but it didn't work out at all for me—I couldn't eat any of the food provided, and the staff was unable to ensure that I got what I needed. So on that particular trip I ate an abundance of grated carrots and white rice.

But on the whole I don't think there are any real problems with traveling, especially for someone like me, who enjoys salads and grilled foods. For example, I order a Greek salad for lunch and then grilled meat with french fries for dinner. These meals are usually always gluten-free, so they're not an issue.

Here are a few simple tips for hassle-free eating when traveling:

★ Clearly explain to the waitstaff of the eating establishment what it means to be gluten intolerant. If this falls on deaf ears, a simple "I will get extremely sick if I eat anything with gluten" will usually get their immediate and undivided attention.

★ If you're a child or teenager, get your parents to interact on your behalf and let them do the explaining. It eases the load a bit when the burden is shared.

★ Don't always trust the chef, especially if his or her attitude is too dismissive and carefree. Dare to be inconvenient and ask to visit the kitchen, just to be on the safe side.

★ Choose a restaurant over a pub. Pub menus are often laden with deep-fried and breaded foods.

★ Sometimes I just don't feel like scrutinizing every last morsel I eat, so I stick to "safe" food. That way I avoid having to go over long lists of ingredients or getting involved in drawn-out discussions with waiters about what selections are gluten-free.

I once visited a fair and when lunchtime rolled around, what I ended up eating may have been the most disgusting meal I have ever had. When I explained that I was gluten intolerant, I was pointed in the direction of what was called an "allergy box," which was "egg, gluten, lactose, nut, tomato, fish, soy, and onion free." I had to heat it myself in a microwave just to make sure that it was totally gluten-free. When I opened that "allergy-box," all I saw was gray glop with some dried, sorry-looking pieces of chicken and a pile of whole-grain rice. Absolutely gross!

Tips! When I'm at a restaurant, I usually select two items that strike my fancy and look gluten-free. I then ask the waitstaff if either of these items are gluten-free, and if not, if it's possible to make a gluten-free version for me. That way I can choose exactly what I want without having to stress out over the order or analyze the entire menu.

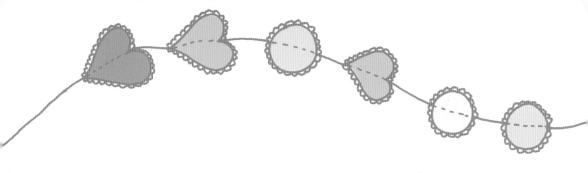

Other treats

These small treats fit so nicely between two fingers and are perhaps the prettiest baked goods in the whole book. The chocolate squares with hazelnuts are my personal faves!

Chocolate Balls

makes approximately 15 balls

YOU'LL NEED:
½ cup (100 g) butter, at room temperature
2 tbsp cocoa powder
4 tbsp granulated sugar
⅔ cup (105 g) rolled oats (PURE oats!)
1 tbsp Nutella hazelnut chocolate spread
1 tbsp fudge sauce

Garnish:
Pearl sugar, shredded coconut, or sprinkles

HOW TO'S:

1. You'll need two dinner plates for this recipe. Pour pearl sugar, shredded coconut, or sprinkles onto one of the plates; use the other one to hold the completed chocolate balls.

2. Pour all ingredients, except your garnish, in a bowl and knead them into a ball of dough.

3. Pinch off a piece of dough and roll it into a ball. Roll the ball in pearl sugar, shredded coconut, or sprinkles and then place it on the second plate.

4. Pinch off pieces of dough to make balls until all the dough is used up and you have a plate full of chocolate balls.

5. Place the plate in the refrigerator to let the treats firm up (if you can wait that long), or simply enjoy them right away.

Nutty Rusks

makes about 30 rusks

I usually make a double batch of these crisp nutty rusks and keep them in a beautiful tin so I can help myself to one whenever a craving hits.

YOU'LL NEED:

¼ cup (32 g) almonds
¼ cup (20 g) walnuts
¼ cup (30 g) hazelnuts
2 large eggs
½ cup (95 g) granulated sugar
½ tsp whole psyllium husk, unflavored
1 cup (150 g) gluten-free flour mix
2 tsp baking powder

HOW TO'S:

1. Preheat a convection oven to 430°F (225°C).
2. Line a cookie sheet with parchment paper.
3. Chop the almonds and nuts coarsely and grind together in a food processor.
4. With a handheld electric mixer, beat the eggs and sugar until light and fluffy.
5. Add in the psyllium husk, gluten-free flour mix, baking powder, almonds, and nuts.
6. Stir with a spoon until you have a batter.
7. Form the batter into two long logs on the cookie sheet.
8. Bake on the middle rack of the oven for about 7 minutes; the lengths will rise and brown a bit.
9. Take the logs out of the oven; let them cool a little, but don't turn off the oven.
10. Cut the lengths on the diagonal, approximately ¾" (3 cm) thick. If the logs are wide, you can even slice them down the middle.
11. Place each rusk, cut surface up, on the cookie sheet.
12. Leave the cookie sheet in the oven for about 3 minutes, until the rusks have gotten some more color.
13. Turn off the oven and open the door slightly to leave it ajar. Keep the rusks in the oven until the oven has cooled down completely. The rusks will be ready when the oven is cool.

Tips! If you've gone trick-or-treating and have collected a lot of candy that you can't eat, weigh the candy and sell it to your parents! For example, if you have 10½ oz (300 g) candy, charge your parents the cost of 10½ oz (300 g) candy, and use the proceeds to go and buy your favorite, gluten-free candy.

Chocolate Squares with Hazelnuts

makes approximately 35 cookies

Seriously, these are the best cookies ever!

YOU'LL NEED:
⅔ cup (90 g) hazelnuts (filberts)
½ cup (100 g) butter
¾ cup (145 g) granulated sugar
1 large egg
⅔ cup (90 g) gluten-free flour mix
2 tbsp cocoa powder
1 tbsp vanilla extract + 1 tbsp sugar

HOW TO'S:
1. Preheat a convection oven to 430°F (225°C).
2. Line a baking pan with high sides with parchment paper. It's best if the paper goes up the sides a bit to prevent the batter from bubbling over while baking.
3. Coarsely chop the hazelnuts. I like them best when they are not too finely ground.
4. Melt the butter for about 1 minute on medium power in the microwave.
5. With a handheld electric mixer, whisk the sugar and eggs until they are light and fluffy.
6. Pour in the butter and whisk until the butter and egg batter are thoroughly mixed.
7. Add the gluten-free flour mix, cocoa powder, vanilla extract, and sugar to the batter. Mix with a spoon until the batter is smooth.
8. Spread the batter in an even rectangle measuring about 8" x 12" (20 cm x 30 cm). Sprinkle with the hazelnuts.
9. Bake on the middle rack of the oven for about 10 minutes, and then let cool a little.
10. Cut the baked cookie dough into diagonally cut squares, to whatever size you prefer.

Tips! *Serve the chocolate squares with a cold glass of milk on a beautiful summer's day or with a cup of hot chocolate on a chilly fall evening.*

A kitchen scale is a must-have when you want to bake macarons. A candy thermometer is also a very handy tool.

Macarons

makes about 15 cookies

Hang on to your hat, because here we have two recipes that are a bit more drawn out and complex than the others. However, these cookies are so amazing that you should not let that scare you off. The recipe for chocolate macarons is the more straightforward of the two, so if you have never tried baking these treats before, I urge you start with them before you attempt the recipe for raspberry flavored ones.

CHOCOLATE MACARONS

YOU'LL NEED:

⅔ cup (80 g) almond flour

1⅓ cup (170 g) confectioner's sugar

⅓ cup (30 g) cocoa powder

⅓ cup (90 g) egg whites

2 tbsp granulated sugar

Filling:

2 tbsp. Nutella hazelnut chocolate spread

⅓ cup (150 g) butter, at room temperature

⅔ cup (60 g) confectioner's sugar

1 tbsp vanilla extract + 1 tbsp sugar

1½ tbsp cocoa powder

HOW TO'S:

1. Preheat a convection oven to 300°F (150°C).
2. Line a cookie sheet with parchment paper.
3. Sift the almond flour, confectioner's sugar, and cacoa into a bowl.
4. Mix thoroughly with a spoon until the mixture is thoroughly combined.
5. With a handheld electric mixer, beat the egg whites until stiff peaks form. When you're able to turn the bowl upside down without the whites sliding out, gradually start adding in the sugar, a little bit at a time, and continue beating until you have a shiny, thick meringue.
6. Combine the meringue with the flour mix very carefully with a spoon. It should not end up fluffy like a pure meringue batter, but more like between a meringue and a sponge cake batter.
7. Spoon the batter into a pastry bag, and pipe the batter into dollops the size of a silver dollar and ⅛" (4 mm) high onto the cookie sheet.
8. Let the cookies rest for at least 30 minutes. This step is critical, because otherwise the cookies will crack in the oven and turn out ugly.
9. Bake the cookies on the lowest rack of the oven for about 12–15 minutes. They'll be ready when they can be easily removed from the parchment paper.
10. Prepare the filling while the cookies are baking: Melt the Nutella in the microwave and then, using a handheld electric mixer, whisk together all the ingredients for the filling. It will look like a powder to start, but with consistent whisking it will turn into a smooth, shiny, and firm cream.
11. Fill a pastry bag with the filling.
12. Remove the cookies from the oven and let them cool.
13. Pair up the cookies, making sure they match each other as closely as possible in size and shape.
14. Pipe a layer of chocolate cream filling on the bottom of one cookie. Press the matching cookie onto the layer of filling to make the treat look like a minihamburger.

RASPBERRY MACARONS

YOU'LL NEED:

1¼ cups (150 g) almond flour
1¼ cups (150 g) confectioner's sugar
¼ cup (60 g) egg whites

Plus

¼ cup (60 g) egg whites
¼ cup (35 g) granulated sugar

Sugar syrup:

¾ cup (150 g) granulated sugar
¼ cup (48 g / 50 ml) water
A few drops of red food coloring

Filling:

Approx 4 oz (100 g) fresh raspberries
1¼ cup (120 g) confectioner's sugar
1 tbsp vanilla pudding mix (cooked, not
    instant)
1 tbsp heavy whipping cream
½ cup (100 g) butter, at room temperature
1 oz (30 g) Philadelphia cream cheese
1¼ cup (120 g) confectioner's sugar

HOW TO'S:

1. Preheat a convection oven to 300°F
   (150°C) and line a cookie sheet with
   parchment paper.
2. Sift the almond flour and
   confectioner's sugar into a bowl. Add
   ¼ cup (60 g) egg whites.
3. Mix thoroughly with a spoon until you
   have light yellow, thick yet smooth cream.
4. In a separate bowl and with a
   handheld electric mixer, beat the other
   ¼ cup (60 g) egg whites until stiff
   peaks form. Add in the sugar when you
   can turn the bowl upside down without
   the egg whites sliding out of the bowl.
   Add the sugar gradually, and continue
   beating until you have a thick, shiny
   meringue batter.
5. Measure out the ingredients for the
   sugar syrup into a saucepan and bring
   them to a boil. Use a candy thermometer
   to check the temperature of the syrup,
   and when it reads 244.4°F (118°C),
   remove the saucepan from the heat.
6. Pour the syrup quickly but carefully
   in a thin stream into the meringue
   batter. Beat with the electric mixer
   about 5 minutes, until the meringue is
   thick, shiny, and totally cooled down.
7. Mix the meringue batter with the
   almond batter. You can do this by
   using the electric mixer on its lowest
   setting for a *short* while to remove
   any lumps. This batter is not meant to
   be fluffy like a true meringue batter,
   but more like something between a
   meringue and sponge cake batter.
8. Place the batter in a pastry bag and
   pipe out rounds the size of a silver
   dollar, approximately ⅛" (4 mm) high,
   onto the cookie sheet.
9. Let the cookies rest for at least 30
   minutes. This step is critical, because
   otherwise the cookies will crack in the
   oven and come out ugly.
10. Bake the cookies on the lowest rack in the
    oven for about 12–15 minutes. They'll be
    ready when they can be easily removed
    from the parchment paper.
11. Prepare the filling while the cookies
    are still in the oven. Start by mashing
    the raspberries in a bowl with the back
    of a spoon.

12. Press the mashed raspberry purée through a sieve and save the juice.
13. Measure up ⅓ cup (75 ml) of the raspberry juice in a saucepan and mix it with the confectioner's sugar.
14. Heat the raspberry juice and confectioner's sugar until it starts to simmer. Pull it from the heat and add in the vanilla pudding powder.
15. Place the saucepan back on the burner and bring the mixture to a boil. It's very important that you keep stirring the contents continuously so they don't scorch. When the mixture has simmered for a while and has thickened substantially, remove the saucepan from the heat and place it carefully in a bowl, or in the sink, filled with ice-cold water.
16. Stir until the mixture is completely cold. It should look like red syrup.
17. Once the syrup is cold, add in the whipping cream. This is done to stop the syrup from gelling too firmly.
18. In a separate bowl and with a handheld electric mixer, beat together the butter, cream cheese, and second measurement of confectioner's sugar. Pour in the raspberry syrup and beat until it becomes a shiny, smooth cream. You can add in some red food coloring if you'd like some more color.
19. Spoon the filling into a pastry bag.
20. Remove the cookies from the oven and let them cool down.
21. Pair up the cookies and make sure they match each other as closely as possible in size and shape.
22. Pipe a layer of raspberry filling on the bottom of one cookie. Press the matching cookie into the filling to form a treat that looks like a minihamburger.

Tips! If the filling separates (that can happen now and again), mix it with an immersion blender and you'll see the filling come together again.

Tips! If you can't find almond flour at the store, buy whole, blanched almonds. Grind them in a nut grinder, Magic Bullet, food processor, or blender. Let the powder dry out overnight and then sift it through a fine meshed sieve. This makes for a bit of extra work. You'll need lots of almonds and you'll lose a fair amount when you sift out the big clumps, but in the end it really does work!

To all near and dear

Are you close to someone who suffers from gluten intolerance? If so, you've turned to the right page. This book is very much directed—as you may already have noticed—to those who've already been given the diagnosis. I'm devoting this particular section, however, to you and to others who put in the added effort to provide us *Glutens* with special meals. First, I want to say "THANK YOU!" because it means so much to us that you care enough to cook that extra pot of gluten-free spaghetti, or keep gluten-free muesli on hand for snacks. I know it's not always easy to extend meal invitations to someone with serious food sensitivities, especially if you yourself can eat just about anything and never deal with special diets. To make things easier for you, I have three helpful tips to share:

1 Keep it simple. It's far easier to prepare salmon with rice, which is naturally gluten-free, than to go hunting for gluten-free pasta and then prepare a meat sauce to go with it.

2 It's the small but thoughtful details that count for so much. Something as uncomplicated as buying a gluten-free loaf of bread for a snack or to go with a meal is what makes us really grateful.

3 Let your gluten-intolerant guests know that you intend to prepare a gluten-free meal. That will give you extra cred in their eyes because then they don't need to worry.

Tips! *Once school is out for the day I'm usually totally starving, but if I go to a friend's place directly after class this can cause issues. The two most popular after-school snacks—sandwiches and cereals—are typically loaded with gluten, so I've solved this problem by leaving a frozen gluten-free loaf of bread and a box of gluten-free cereal at my best friends' homes. That way I always have something tasty to eat when I'm with them. Otherwise there's always fruit, which is naturally gluten-free.*

Did you know that many have chosen to eat a gluten-free diet, even though they aren't gluten intolerant? They do it because it's healthier.

Tips! *A bowl of cultured buttermilk or yogurt sprinkled with nuts and raisins makes a great snack if you don't have anything specifically gluten-free in the house. Drizzle over some honey— scrumptious!*

Snacks

heck out the recipes in this chapter on afternoons when you want to whip up something quick and yummy. My favorite, which I've made hundreds of times, is the apple salad.

Raspberry Smoothie

This is one of my standby snacks, but it also makes a great breakfast.

YOU'LL NEED:
1¼ cups (160 g) frozen raspberries
1¼ cups (300 ml) vanilla yogurt
1 banana
3 tsp vanilla extract + 3 tsp sugar

HOW TO'S:
1. Pour all the ingredients in a blender or in a bowl with high sides.
2. Blend. You might have to stir with a spoon if the raspberries clump.
3. Pour into two glasses and serve immediately.

Tips! You can occasionally splatter quite a bit when you're mixing or blending, so make sure to put the lid on the blender, or use a plate as a splatter guard if you are mixing in a bowl.

Turbo Sorbet

A super simple recipe for a fresh homemade sorbet!

YOU'LL NEED:
2 cups (250 g) frozen mango
2 cups (250 g) frozen raspberries
⅔ cup (60 g) confectioner's sugar

HOW TO'S:
1. Leave the mango and raspberries at room temperature to thaw out gradually, or defrost them faster in the microwave.
2. Place the thawed mango and raspberries with the confectioner's sugar in a food processor. Process until you have a smooth sorbet. I like it when there are still a few chunks of fruit left.
3. Taste and add some additional confectioner's sugar if you find it necessary.
4. Enjoy immediately!

Apple Salad with Rolled Oats

I put together this treat with my pals Alma and Tove one fall afternoon when we were really hungry and our apple trees were full of fruit. It tastes a bit like an unbaked apple pie and is the perfect snack when you're at someone's house where he or she doesn't keep gluten-free foods. We often make this salad, and our record so far for apples eaten in one sitting has been 21!

YOU'LL NEED:

2 apples
1 tsp ground cinnamon
1½ tbsp honey
¼ cup (35 g) rolled oats (make sure they're pure oats!)

HOW TO'S:

1. Core the apples and dice them into small cubes. The smaller the pieces are diced, the tastier the salad.
2. Place the apple dice into a large bowl. Dust with cinnamon and shake the bowl to evenly distribute the cinnamon over the apple pieces.
3. Drizzle the honey over the apples and cinnamon, and mix thoroughly until all the apple pieces are a bit sticky.
4. Add in the rolled oats. Stir until everything is evenly mixed.
5. Eat immediately.

About oats: Oats are naturally gluten-free, but they can be contaminated through contact with other cereals. If you're gluten intolerant, it's very important to use pure oats (which have not been processed in a facility that processes products that contain gluten; check the label on the package carefully). You'll find them in the grocery aisle devoted to gluten-free products.

Scones

makes 2 large or 4 small scones

YOU'LL NEED:
2 cups (270 g) gluten-free flour mix
2 tsp baking powder
1¾ oz (50 g) butter
6¾ fl oz (200 ml) milk

1 egg, for glazing

HOW TO'S:
1. Preheat a convection oven to 480°F (250°C).
2. Line a cookie sheet with parchment paper.
3. Mix the gluten-free flour mix with the baking powder.
4. Cut the butter into small pieces and add it to the flour mixture. Work the butter into the flour—I usually crumble it between my fingers until it's fully incorporated and I can no longer see it. (That's the secret to perfect scones!)
5. Add in the milk and work it all quickly into dough. If the dough is too sticky to handle, add in a tiny amount of the gluten-free flour mix.
6. Shape the dough into 2 large or 4 small round balls, and place them on the prepared cookie sheet.
7. Flatten the scones into ½" (1½ cm) thick rounds. Score each round with a cross, just about halfway through the dough, not straight through. Prick the surface with a fork.
8. Beat the egg to make a wash; brush the top of the scones with the egg wash before sliding them into the oven. (The scones will look very pale if you omit the egg wash.)
9. Bake the scones on the middle rack of the oven for about 10 minutes, or until the scones develop a nice golden color.

Tips! *Serve the scones with tea and an assortment of spreads and other snacks. I usually lay the table with dishes of butter, orange marmalade, raspberry jam, lemon curd, and different cheeses and ham, to go with the scones.*

Sometimes it's just plain boring

"Let food heal you!" How often have you heard that expression? Some people claim we're lucky, that we should feel grateful that we're simply gluten intolerant. In our case it's only a matter of eating right and we'll feel OK, unlike diabetics who need medication and injections.

However, it's not always easy—or fun—to "just eat right." Especially when there's a coffee table laid out with a platter of irresistibly aromatic and fresh cinnamon rolls and you have to merely sit there with a glass of soda, or if you're lucky, a bun—often one of those frozen, prepackaged, dry things. Or when everyone in Home Economics is making apple pie but the teacher has forgotten to bring gluten-free flour mix. Or in the cafeteria at school, where the gluten-free food takes so long to arrive that your friends have almost finished their lunches by the time you sit down with your food.

I remember clearly the moment I learned I was gluten intolerant: I was in the bathtub, and my mom came in to the bathroom to tell me that she had talked to Dr. Anders, who had received the test results that indicated I was gluten intolerant.

I was too young to understand what that meant; I only realized that I was now different from others. On top of which, I was given weird foods to eat and could no longer be treated to cakes or cookies when we stopped at a coffee shop. When my parents explained to me that this was not a temporary thing but was to be my new way of life, it did make my existence feel a little lackluster.

With this book, however, I want to prove that being gluten intolerant doesn't necessarily mean you have to lead a bland or restricted life. It's true that this condition can occasionally be tedious or irritating, but that's part of life, isn't it?

Tips! *I have my own gluten-free cupboard where you'll only find gluten-free products. Everything is kept in one designated place.*

Tips!

At home, I have my own toaster, toaster oven, and my own separate packet of butter. That way there's no risk of me coming into contact with foods that contain gluten when I make my sandwiches.

Tips! *I keep two small bags—one with pasta and one with muesli —in my locker at school. That way I always have something to eat if I go home with a friend when I have a longer break during the school day.*

Savory baked goods

In here you'll find baked goods that taste savory, not sweet—the kind of foods our moms and dads would approve of us baking. In my opinion, the best recipe is probably the one for the pizza buns because it's simply a brilliant idea to combine buns and pizza.

Pancakes

makes about 4 to 5 pancakes

The first time I tasted pancakes was when I visited a family friend, called Miko, on the Swedish island of Gotland, and he prepared this amazing brunch. Since then I've become totally devoted—I love these!

YOU'LL NEED:
2 large eggs
6¾ fl oz (200 ml) milk
¾ cup (120 g) gluten-free flour mix
2 tsp baking powder
½ tsp salt
Butter, for frying

Suggested toppings:
Butter
Maple syrup
Blueberries
Bacon

HOW TO'S:
1. You'll need three different bowls.
2. Separate the egg whites from the yolks; put the whites in the first bowl and the yolks in the second.
3. Use a handheld electric mixer and beat the egg whites until stiff peaks form. You should be able to turn the bowl upside down without the whites sliding out.
4. Add the milk to the egg yolks. Whisk with a fork until they are well blended.
5. Combine the gluten-free flour mix, baking powder, and salt in the third bowl. It's important to stir these dry ingredients thoroughly so the baking powder is evenly distributed through the mix. (If not, the pancakes will turn out unevenly—flat on one side and fluffy on the other.)
6. With a handheld electric mixer, beat together the egg batter and gluten-free flour mix until the batter is smooth and free of any lumps.
7. Carefully fold in the beaten egg whites. Don't use the electric mixer here because it will break up the air bubbles of the egg whites. Instead, stir them in carefully with a spoon. The gentler you are, the fluffier the pancakes.
8. Place some butter in a frying pan and turn the heat up to medium high. When the butter starts to bubble and becomes golden, pour in a good dollop of the batter. Don't spread the batter in the pan—just leave it as a large dollop.
9. Fry the pancakes on both sides until they are cooked through. Serve them with your preferred toppings.

Pizza

makes 3 large or 9 small pizzas

It's almost impossible to make a tasty gluten-free pizza if you don't have a good recipe to work from. This one is indeed good. Not bad!

YOU'LL NEED:

¾ cup (200 ml) + ¼ fl oz (50 ml) lukewarm water

1 oz (25 g) cake yeast (or ½ oz active dry yeast)

1 tbsp whole psyllium husk, unflavored

¼ fl oz (50 ml) olive oil

1 tsp salt

2 cups (300 g) gluten-free flour mix

1 tsp baking powder

Some flour mix for working the dough

Topping(s):

Tomato sauce

Grated cheese

And whatever other toppings you like on your pizza!

HOW TO'S:

1. If using cake yeast, mix ¾ cup lukewarm water with the yeast and the whole psyllium husk. It's critical that the water is lukewarm (not too warm, not too cold) or the yeast won't "bloom" properly. (If using dry yeast, follow the directions on the packet.)
2. Add the oil and salt and mix with a fork.
3. Let rise 10 minutes.
4. Add the gluten-free flour mix and the baking powder. Work the dough, preferably with a standing mixer, until it's dry and pretty crumbly. (Don't despair—it will soon be amazing!)
5. Add ¼ fl oz water. Work it into the dough.
6. Preheat a convection oven to 430°F (225°C).
7. Line a cookie sheet with parchment paper.
8. Let the dough rise under a kitchen towel for about 30 minutes.
9. On a floured baking board, roll out the dough to form thin pizza rounds.
10. Spread tomato sauce onto the rounds and add the toppings of your choice. Finish by sprinkling on some grated cheese. I prefer small amounts of toppings because if the pizza is loaded too heavily, it becomes heavy and soggy and the crust will not cook properly.
11. Bake on the upper rack of the oven: 15 minutes for large pizzas and about 8 minutes for small ones. You'll notice when the pizzas are ready!

Tips! Baking mini pizzas is great because you can make several pizzas and try out all sorts of different toppings. What you don't eat right away you can freeze and then defrost later for a snack when the cravings come.

Pizza Buns

makes 20 large buns

These buns are just like the ordinary cinnamon rolls, except these are filled with pizza fixings. They're great for bringing along on a picnic or to eat before sports practice.

YOU'LL NEED:
⅓ cup (75 g) butter
1 cup (250 ml) milk
1 oz (25 g) cake yeast (or ½ oz active dried yeast)
1 tbsp whole psyllium husk, unflavored
1¾ fl oz (50 ml) light syrup
1¾ fl oz (50 ml) filmjölk (available at Whole Foods or specialty stores, or substitute with cultured buttermilk or yogurt) This might sound a bit weird but it adds a great tasting tang to the dough.
1 tsp salt
3 cups (420 g) gluten-free flour mix

Filling:
Tomato sauce
1¼ to 1⅔ cups (120 to 160 g) grated cheese
1 jar of bell-pepper stuffed green olives
5¼ oz (150 g) ham

Some gluten-free flour mix for handling the dough
Bun baking molds

Glazing:
1 large egg

HOW TO'S:
1. Melt the butter in the microwave or in a saucepan on the stovetop.
2. Pour the butter into the liquid ingredients to raise their temperature to lukewarm (not too warm, not too cold). You might have to warm the liquids in the microwave a little to get them to the right temperature, but be very careful to not heat them too much!
3. Crumble the cake yeast into the butter/milk liquid. (If using dried yeast, follow the instructions on the packet*).
4. Add the psyllium husk, stir with a fork, and then let rise for 10 minutes.
5. Place the syrup, cultured buttermilk or yogurt, salt, gluten-free flour mix, and butter/milk liquid in a bowl. With a handheld electric mixer fitted with dough hooks, or a standing mixer with dough hook attachments, work the dough vigorously for about 5 minutes. It's important to work the dough thoroughly to make it smooth and elastic.
6. Let the dough rise 50 minutes under a kitchen towel.
7. Preheat a convection oven to 430°F (225°C).
8. While the dough is rising, grate the cheese, chop the olives, and slice the ham.
9. Knead the dough briefly after it has risen.
10. Sprinkle some flour on the baking board. Roll the dough out into a thin rectangle.
11. Spread the tomato sauce onto the dough; sprinkle the cheese, ham, and olives evenly over the sauce.
12. Roll the dough as if making a Swiss roll, and cut it into 20 even pieces.
13. Place each piece in a baking mold. Press the dough down to make the buns large and a bit flattened, as they will rise in the oven heat.
14. Whisk the egg to make an egg wash, and brush the buns with the wash.
15. Bake the pizza buns on the middle rack of the oven for about 7 minutes.
16. Serve the buns right out of the oven, or freeze them for later.

* Dry yeast isn't handled the same way as fresh yeast and sometimes the instructions from different makers vary, so follow the instructions on the packet carefully.

Homemade Pasta

makes 1 small serving

YOU'LL NEED:

½ cup (75 g) gluten-free flour mix
1 large egg
Some gluten-free flour mix for working the
dough (don't use too much, or it will
make the pasta starchy)

HOW TO'S:

1. Pour the gluten-free flour mix and the egg in a bowl.
2. With a handheld electric mixer with dough hook attachment, work the mix until it starts looking like dough. Knead the dough until there are no more crumbs. It is of utmost importance to knead the dough thoroughly or the pasta will easily fall apart.
3. Place the pasta dough on a floured baking board. Dust the dough with some gluten-free flour mix and roll it out with a rolling pin.
4. Roll the pin back and forth a few times and then turn the dough. Dust the dough again. Roll and dust the dough a few more times until it's thin enough to see straight through it when you hold it up. The thinner the dough, the thinner and—most importantly—the tastier the pasta.
5. Cut the pasta dough into ribbons—as thin or wide as you prefer (I like them about ⅛ inch (3mm) wide). Place the pasta strips on a plate.
6. Bring some salted water with a bit of added olive oil to a boil.
7. Add the pasta when the water is at a rolling boil. Let the pasta cook for 2 minutes.
8. Drain the pasta and serve!

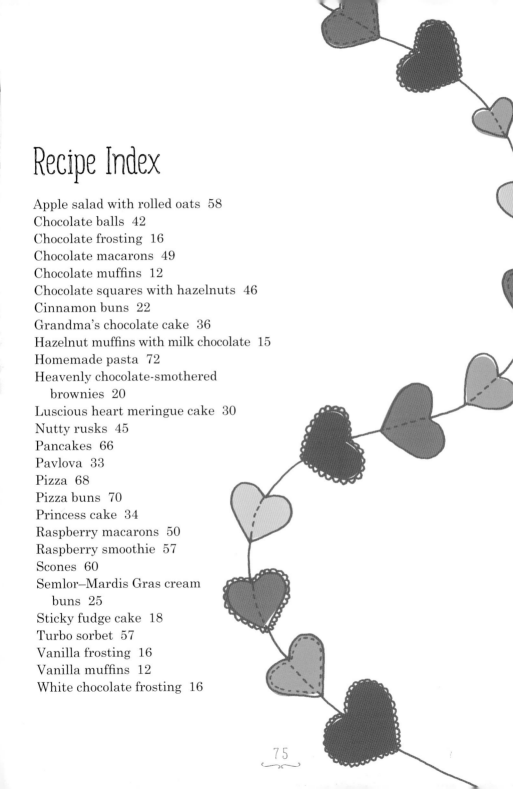

Recipe Index

A big thanks goes to:

The world's coolest photographer, Jenny Grimsgård, who took the most fantastic pictures,

Katy Kimbell, who has an incredible eye for graphics— her illustrations make this book so special—

&

My publisher in Sweden, Sofia Hahr, who is simply the best; throughout this entire process she did not lose sight of me, even though I was only fifteen when this book was first published.

❅

My family, who have always cheered me on and encouraged me to spread my wings, even when that meant being available for taste tests, and who have tried to sleep through the clatter of baking trays and whirring electric mixers in the middle of the night.

My best friends Alma and Emelie, as well as my (sort of) little sister Tuva; they all brightened these pages with their beautiful smiles.

And last, but not least, a heartfelt thank you to everyone who has been there for me. You know who you are.

All of you contributed to making this book a real gem; without you it would never have turned out as nice as it did.

You are the best.

www.skyhorsepublishing.com

10 9 8 7 6 5 4 3 2 1

Library of Congress Cataloging-in-Publication Data is available on file.

ISBN: 978-1-63220-474-5
Ebook ISBN: 978-1-63450-109-5

Cover design by Eric Kang
Cover photos: Jenny Grimsgård
Graphic and Illustration: Katy Kimbell
Printed in China